ART · FROM · THE · PAST

The
VIKINGS

GILLIAN CHAPMAN

GENERAL CRAFT TIPS AND SAFETY PRECAUTIONS

Read the instructions carefully. Then collect together your materials before you start work. Some projects require decoration, and it is best to plan your design first on rough paper.

If you are working with papier mâché or paint, cover your work surface with newspaper.

Ask an adult to help if you are using sharp tools such as a knife or compasses. Use a cutting mat when cutting with a craft knife.

When using and mixing plaster, always follow the manufacturer's instructions on the packet.

Keep paint and glue brushes separate and always wash them after use. PVA glue is fine for sticking paper, card and collage materials.

Don't be impatient: make sure plaster is set and papier mâché and paint is thoroughly dry before moving on to the next stage!

Make sure you wash your hands after mashing paper pulp and glue.

RECYCLING

It's a good idea to continuously collect materials for craftwork. Save newspapers, clean coloured paper and card, cardboard boxes and tubes of different sizes. Scraps of string, old buttons, beads, dried peas and beans are great for collage.

Clean plastic containers and old utensils are perfect for mixing plaster and making paper pulp.

PICTURE CREDITS

The Bridgeman Art Library: 10; **C M Dixon:** 5 bottom and 6 bottom; **Historic Scotland:** 26 above; **Mary Evans Picture Library:** 5 top; **Michael Holford:** 4 top, 6 middle, 26 below; **The National Museum of Denmark:** 12 and 22; **Robert Harding Picture Library:** 14; **Statens Historiska Museum:** 28; **Universitetets Oldsaksamling:** 4 bottom right and 16; **Werner Forman Archive:** 4 bottom left, 5 middle, 6 top, 20 above, 24; **York Archaeological Trust:** 18 and 20 below.

Photographer: Rupert Horrox
Illustrator: Gillian Chapman, Picture Researcher: Jennie Karrach

This edition published in 2006 by Fernleigh Books,
1A London Road, Enfield, Middlesex, EN2 6BN

ISBN 1 905212 39 9

Printed in China

The author and Fernleigh Books would like to thank
Keith Chapman for all his help with the model making.

ART · FROM · THE · PAST

The VIKINGS

GILLIAN CHAPMAN

The Vikings 4

Arts and Crafts 6

Runestones 8

Viking Longships 10

Viking Navigators 12

Dragon Figurehead 14

Warrior Helmets 16

Trading Places 18

Minting Coins 20

Buried Treasure 22

Gods and Amulets 24

Viking Board Game 26

Viking Chieftains 28

Glossary 30

Index 32

Any words appearing in the text in bold, like **this**, are explained in the glossary.

THE VIKINGS

THE VIKINGS were a seafaring and farming people that lived in the lands we know as Norway, Denmark and Sweden. During the late 700s there was a period of rapid population growth in **Scandinavia** and the amount of farmland available to Viking families became smaller. This overcrowding led to family feuds and local conflicts over land. Many Vikings were forced to leave these areas to find places to live elsewhere.

At the same time the Vikings were building strong, fast ships, which enabled them to travel further afield and explore new lands. Soon the Vikings had become the most powerful people in Europe. Their influence stretched far and wide: east across Russia, west to Iceland, Greenland and North America, and south around the Mediterranean and North Africa.

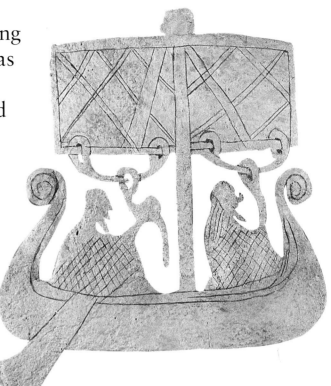

ABOVE. *This Viking ship, with a single sail and steering board, is carved on a **runestone** from Gotland, Sweden.*

BELOW. *In 1880 this Viking ship was excavated from a royal burial mound at Gokstad, Norway.*

BELOW. *A 10th century Danish dragon-head post.*

KINGS, NOBLES AND THE LAW

VIKING SOCIETY was divided into three main classes, the nobles (or chieftains), freemen and slaves. All were ruled by royal families. The nobles were powerful landowners and warriors who gained their wealth by raiding other territories. The freemen were small landowners, farmers, traders and craftsmen. The slaves (or thralls) were often foreigners captured overseas and brought back to Scandinavia to work.

At the beginning of the Viking age many nobles and chieftains ruled over small areas, each having a local assembly, called 'the **Thing**'. Laws and local issues were discussed by the freemen, who had the power to judge crimes and sentence men to death. Eventually governing power fell into the hands of a few nobles who gained it by conquering their neighbours and absorbing their land and wealth. By about AD 1000, the kingdoms of Norway, Sweden and Denmark were each ruled independently by their own king.

ABOVE. *This fantastic 19th century painting of a Viking warrior incorrectly shows him wearing a helmet with horns.*

ABOVE RIGHT. *A carved wooden head found in the royal burial ship at Oseberg, Norway.*

RIGHT. *A meeting of the Icelandic Althing in AD 1000.*

ARTS AND CRAFTS

VIKING CRAFT WORKERS were extremely good at making tools. The vast **Scandinavian** forests gave them plentiful supplies of wood to make furniture, wagons, ships and everyday objects. Wood, antlers and bone were carved with wonderful mythological beasts and serpents linked together in twisting patterns. Metal workers and blacksmiths were highly respected. They used their skills to make weapons, especially sharp blades, that the Viking warriors prized. Many also made delicate jewellery, brooches and clasps, using precious metals imported from the East.

ABOVE. *This wooden panel from an 11th century church at Hylestad in Norway shows a blacksmith at work.*

The Viking runic script was known by only a few stone carvers. They carved inscriptions on large memorial stones to honour brave warriors or great events. These **runestones** tell their stories in a series of pictures and **runes** and can be found throughout Scandinavia.

ABOVE. *A mythological beast carved on a Viking tombstone, found in the churchyard of St Paul's Cathedral, London.*

LEFT. *This 11th century Swedish runestone was erected by a woman named Astrid in memory of her husband Oysten 'who went to Jerusalem and died in Greekland'.*

Viking Craft Tips

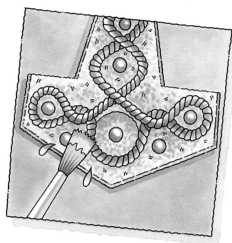

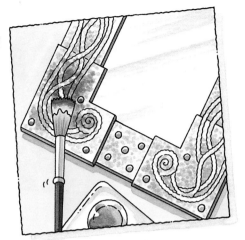

Use poster paints to paint the Viking projects. Poster paints are water-based, easy to mix and use, and will give the projects bright, strong colours.

Poster paints are also available in metallic colours such as bronze, silver and gold. These are perfect for making projects resemble metal.

To give projects a tarnished look, mix the metallic paint with black poster paint to give a darker shade and brush this onto the surface.

Dowels are lengths of round wood used in craft work. They are made from pine or balsa wood, are easy to work with and can be bought from most DIY or craft shops.

Attach a split pin by piercing through the card first with a sharp pencil or compass point, to make a small hole. Once you have folded back the pin tabs, cover them with sticky tape.

Some Viking projects use collage materials to make raised designs and textures. We've used coiled strings, split peas, small buttons and pieces of tissue.

RUNESTONES

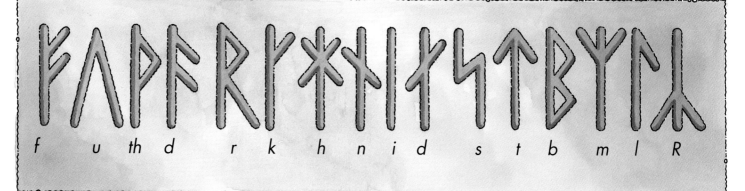

f u th d r k h n i d s t b m l R

THE VIKING PEOPLES of **Scandinavia** used an alphabet made from **rune** characters, called the futhark. Each rune is formed from straight lines or vertical and diagonal lines, making them very easy to carve. Most surviving runic inscriptions exist on stone monuments, called **runestones**. However they were also carved on wood, weapons and jewellery.

The word 'rune' comes from the Gothic word meaning secret. Runes were shrouded in mystery because very few people could read or understand them and each rune may have had several meanings. The futhark shown above was used by the Danes; the Norwegian and Swedish Vikings had different versions of the alphabet.

RUNESTONE BOOKENDS

1. First make the two card moulds. Take one piece of strong card and measure a 5cm wide strip around each side. Cut away the corners (as shown).

2. Score along the lines with the scissor tips. Turn up the sides and secure them with tape. Repeat with the second piece of card to make the other mould.

3. Mix up the plaster in an old plastic container, following the instructions on the packet. Pour the plaster into the moulds, smooth over the surface and leave to dry.

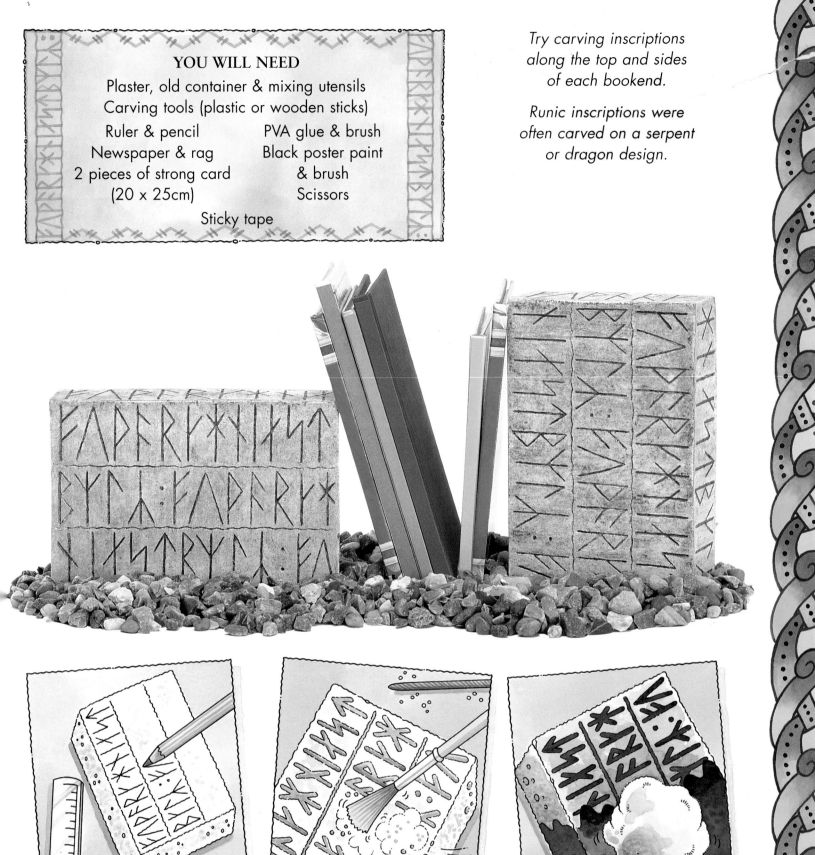

YOU WILL NEED

Plaster, old container & mixing utensils
Carving tools (plastic or wooden sticks)
Ruler & pencil   PVA glue & brush
Newspaper & rag   Black poster paint
2 pieces of strong card   & brush
(20 x 25cm)   Scissors

Sticky tape

Try carving inscriptions along the top and sides of each bookend.

Runic inscriptions were often carved on a serpent or dragon design.

4. When the plaster is dry, tear off the moulds. Use the pencil to divide the front of each bookend into three. Then copy the runic alphabet in rows, onto the plaster.

5. Use the carving tools to carve the runes into the plaster. Brush out all the dust from the carved lines before painting the surface with a thin coat of diluted PVA.

6. Paint over the surface, making sure the paint fills all the carved lines. Carefully wipe all the excess paint from the surface with a damp rag, but leave it in the carved lines.

VIKING LONGSHIPS

THE VIKINGS were the greatest seamen of their time, building narrow warships up to 30 metres long. The wood most commonly used was oak or pine cut from the vast Scandinavian forests. The **longships** had a **keel** which made them more stable and easy to steer, enabling the Vikings to travel great distances without stopping. At sea the ships were powered by the wind. A flexible pine mast supported the large woollen sail. On rivers the Viking warriors rowed the ships. A longship could have up to 50 oars.

The Vikings were surrounded by the sea. Hundreds of **fjords** cut into their coastline and boats were the main form of transport.

YOU WILL NEED
Poster paints, palette & brush
Craft knife & cutting board

15 x 35cm brown card	PVA glue & brush
18 x 3cm brown card	Scissors
2 x 22cm dowels	20cm square sail
Blunt needle & thread	Thin white card
Split pins	Pencil

LONGSHIP

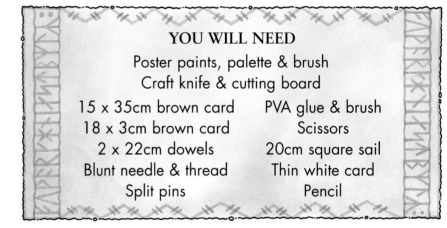

1. Take the 15 x 35cm piece of brown card and paint a wooden plank design along the length. Leave to dry. Fold the card in half and cut the ends into a curved boat shape.

2. Divide the 18 x 3cm card strip into sections as shown. Use the craft knife to cut a star shape in the centre of the smaller sections. Fold the card to make the mast support.

3. Glue the base of the ship together along the curved edges and leave to dry. Then open the long edge and glue the mast support between the two sides of the base.

10

4. Paint both sides of the sail with stripes. Draw 5cm diameter shields, a 12cm long steering board, and 7cm long prow and stern shapes onto thin card. Paint and cut them out.

5. Place the top end of one dowel across the centre of the second. Bind them together with thread and blobs of glue. Then glue the horizontal dowel to the top of the sail.

6. Glue the prow and stern in place on both sides. Attach the shields to both sides and the steering board to the front of the ship with split pins. Push the sail dowel into the mast support.

*The large steering board, or rudder, was always on the right side of the ship. To avoid damaging it the opposite side of the boat was always moored up in port, and these are the origins of the terms 'port' and **'starboard'**. Try sewing extra **rigging** to the sail to make it look even more realistic!*

VIKING NAVIGATORS

EARLY VOYAGES ACROSS the Atlantic are described in the Viking **sagas**, which give detailed sailing instructions for journeys from Norway to Greenland and North America. Mountains on the Shetland Islands, glaciers on Greenland, and birds and whales off Iceland were all described. If the sailors could not find land, they released ravens and followed the direction the birds flew. The raven was an important Viking symbol and appeared on their flags.

This fragment of a **sun compass** dial has survived and the illustration shows how the sun compass dial would have looked.

SUN COMPASS

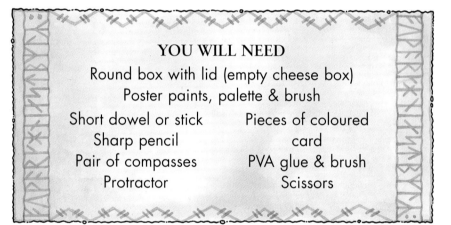

YOU WILL NEED
Round box with lid (empty cheese box)
Poster paints, palette & brush
Short dowel or stick   Pieces of coloured
Sharp pencil   card
Pair of compasses   PVA glue & brush
Protractor   Scissors

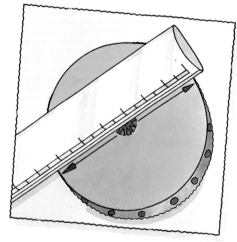

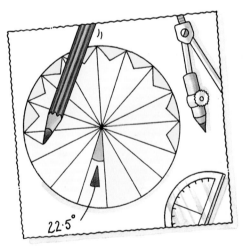

22.5°

1. Make a small hole with the compass point in the centre of the lid and base of the box. Carefully push the sharp pencil through to enlarge the holes in the box.

2. Glue the box together with the PVA glue. Paint the box with poster paints, leave to dry and glue card circles to the side. Use the ruler to measure the diameter of the box.

3. Use the compass to draw a circle on the card the same diameter as the box. Then use the protractor to divide the circle into 16 sections, or points of the compass.

4. Cut out the card compass and enlarge the centre hole using the sharp pencil. Glue the shape onto the box. Push the wooden dowel through the centre and secure with PVA.

5. Cut out a smaller circle of card and enlarge the centre hole with the sharp pencil. Attach a card pointer to the circle and slip it over the dowel.

The pointer should turn freely. Hold the compass with the bottom part of the dowel.

Viking explorers used the sun and stars to navigate the sea. They would have recorded the position of the sun's shadow over several years. Using this knowledge, they could measure the height of the sun above the horizon from the shadow cast on the sun compass. This would make it possible to calculate latitude, which was their north/south position. The sun's shadow points to a compass direction and the pointer shows the ship's course.

The Vikings usually sailed in sight of land. The sun compass was one of the tools they used on long sea voyages, but it could only be used on sunny days.

On overcast days the Vikings would use their knowledge of the winds, tides and wave patterns, and sightings of sea birds and animals, to get their bearings.

DRAGON FIGUREHEAD

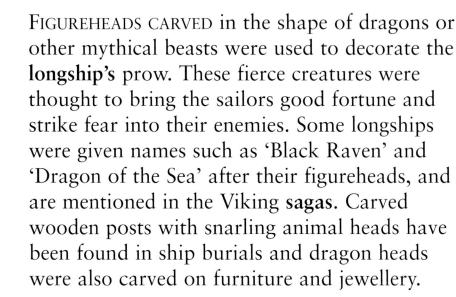

FIGUREHEADS CARVED in the shape of dragons or other mythical beasts were used to decorate the **longship's** prow. These fierce creatures were thought to bring the sailors good fortune and strike fear into their enemies. Some longships were given names such as 'Black Raven' and 'Dragon of the Sea' after their figureheads, and are mentioned in the Viking **sagas**. Carved wooden posts with snarling animal heads have been found in ship burials and dragon heads were also carved on furniture and jewellery.

DRAGON FRAME

YOU WILL NEED

Small mirror	Scissors
Strong card	PVA glue & brush
Craft knife	String & split peas
Cutting board	Silver poster paint
Paper & pencil	& brush
Ruler	Black poster paint

1. Glue the mirror to the centre of the thick card with PVA and leave to dry. Use the craft knife and ruler to trim away the excess card around the mirror, leaving a 4cm margin.

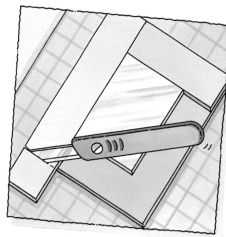

2. Build up the frame around the mirror with four 4cm card strips. Trim the pieces and glue in place. To stand the mirror up, glue a 6cm wide card strip to the back of the frame.

3. Draw four 'L' shaped pieces on the card. These should all be 6cm wide to fit each corner of the frame. Cut these out and glue into place over the frame.

The small square frame is made using square corners instead of 'L' shaped ones.

Many Viking designs include dragons and coiled patterns.

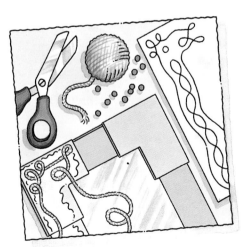

4. Sketch a dragon design for the frame on paper. Spread a thin layer of glue over part of the frame, follow the design and begin to glue pieces of string to the card.

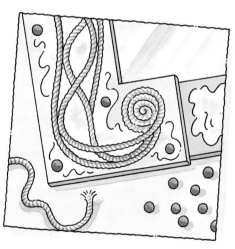

5. Use the split peas to build up the raised pattern over the whole frame. Leave areas to dry before continuing further. Make sure all the pieces are glued down firmly.

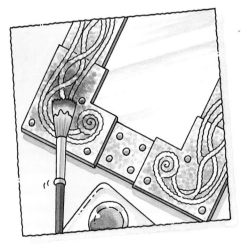

6. Paint the frame with silver paint. To make it look old and tarnished, mix some black paint with the silver and lightly brush it over the frame (see Craft Tips on page 7).

WARRIOR HELMETS

THE VIKINGS acquired a fiercesome reputation, because of their violent raids and surprise attacks on peaceful settlements. The expression 'to go a-viking' meant to fight like a pirate and warrior. The word 'viking' referred to young men seeking adventure overseas. Many Scandinavians did 'go a-viking', but the majority were peaceful farmers, traders and craft workers.

Only wealthy Viking leaders wore **chain mail** and helmets of iron and leather, and warriors never wore horns on their helmets.

This Viking helmet is made of iron plates, welded together, with nose and eye guards.

LEATHER HELMET

YOU WILL NEED
Head-sized blown-up balloon
Newspaper
PVA glue & brush
Round bowl
Thin card & scissors
Bronze & silver poster paint & brush
Split pins
Black poster paint
Tape measure

1. To make the helmet shape, glue torn newspaper pieces over the top half of the blown-up balloon with diluted PVA glue.

2. Support the balloon in a bowl and continue to cover the top part of the balloon with six more layers of newspaper. Leave the balloon to dry and then pop it.

3. Trim around the bottom of the helmet shape with scissors to neaten the edge. Paint the helmet with the bronze poster paint and leave to dry.

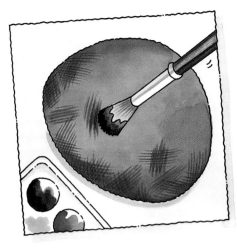  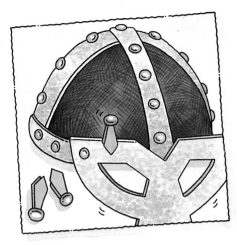

4. To make the helmet look like it is made of leather, lightly brush the black poster paint over the painted surface, making sure the bronze paint shows through.

5. Cut out some narrow strips of thin card, long enough to stretch around the helmet. Draw the eye guard shape on the thin card, cut it out and paint all the shapes silver.

6. Attach the strips and the eye guard to the helmet with the split pins. Paint all the silver shapes and split pins with black and silver paint to make them look like iron.

*The most ferocious Viking warriors were called **'berserkers'**. They wore only bearskin cloaks and worked themselves into a mad frenzy before battle.*

Viking warriors were fearless fighters whose greatest glory was to die in battle.

For extra advice about attaching split pins and using metallic paints, see Craft Tips on page 7.

17

TRADING PLACES

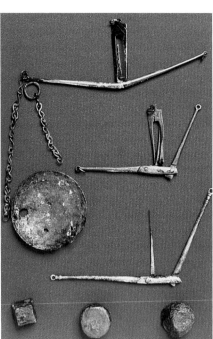

THE VIKINGS were great traders who travelled far beyond **Scandinavia**. They sailed along river routes into Russia and Central Asia. Their most valuable export was slaves, captured during raids. They also traded furs, timber and iron for gold, silver, wine, salt and exotic spices from the East.

At first Vikings exchanged goods, because coins came into use much later, but they also traded using silver. Merchants carried sets of small scales with them to weigh broken pieces of silver coins and jewellery.

Scales like these have been found all over the Viking world.

TRADER'S SCALES

YOU WILL NEED

Poster paints, palette & brush	22 x 4cm balsa wood & some adult help
7 x 25cm lengths of string	3 x beads
2 x round card boxes (empty cheese boxes)	Blunt needle
	Scissors
Single hole punch	Self-hardening clay & modelling tools
Ruler	Use of kitchen scales

1. Use the single hole punch to make three holes, equal distance apart, in the rim of the box's lid and base. Then paint designs onto the lid and base.

2. Ask an adult to make three holes in the balsa wood bar – one hole in the centre and one 1.5cm from each end. Then paint the bar with designs to match the box.

3. Tie a length of string through each hole in the lid. Thread each length with the needle, pass them through a hole in the bar's end, through a bead and tie them together.

Hold the scales by the central string and use them to weigh out your goods.

4. Repeat for the other side. Thread the needle with the last piece of string, tie a knot at one end and pass the needle through the bead and centre hole. Tie a loop at the end.

5. Make a series of weights for the scales from self-hardening clay. Use kitchen scales to make each weight twice as big as the last. Scratch a different design on each weight and leave them to dry before painting.

Use a second round box to make a container for your weights. Paint it to match your set of scales.

Viking traders used small portable scales that folded up into a case, making them easy to carry.

MINTING COINS

At first the Vikings traded goods by **barter**, with any differences in the value of goods made up in silver coins. The coins came from the many different countries that the Vikings traded with and were valued by their weight. Silver coins were quite soft and could be cut into small pieces to make up exact values.

Coins were made using a metal die stamp that punched the coin design into metal. This die (left) was found at the Viking town of **Jorvik** (York).

Popular designs for coins included ships, animals and buildings.

DIE STAMP AND COINS

YOU WILL NEED
Metallic & coloured poster paints & brush
Pack of self-hardening clay

Plastic or wooden carving tools & board for rolling out clay
Rolling pin
Card tube & scissors

PVA glue & brush
20 x 10cm piece of felt
String, needle & thread for the bag

1. To make the die stamp, mould the clay with your hands. Roll it into a bottle shape, with a wide base and narrow handle. Keep the surface as smooth as possible.

2. Flatten the base of the stamp by gently pushing it down onto the board. Cut a 2cm ring from a card tube and push it into the base, leaving at least 1cm sticking out.

3. Decorate the handle of the die stamp with patterns or carve your initials using the carving tools. Be careful when handling the stamp not to squash your design.

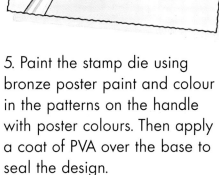

4. Use the carving tools to draw a simple picture or design in the clay in the centre of the ring. The design will be the markings on the coin. Leave the clay die to harden.

5. Paint the stamp die using bronze poster paint and colour in the patterns on the handle with poster colours. Then apply a coat of PVA over the base to seal the design.

6. Roll out some more clay, about 1cm thick, and use the die stamp to punch out some coins. Leave the coins to harden before painting with metallic paints.

To make the money bag, fold the felt in half and sew it together along two sides. Make small holes around the opening with the scissor tips and thread the string through.

Make a range of coins and paint them in gold, silver and bronze paints.

21

BURIED TREASURE

VIKING KINGS, chiefs and warriors who distinguished themselves in battle were buried with great honour. The wealthiest men and women were buried in **ship graves** with **hoards** of treasure to accompany them on their journey to the afterlife. Warriors were sometimes buried with swords and armour, noblemen might be buried with servants and animals.

'Grave goods' of gold and silver, beautiful vessels and tools were made specially to be buried with the dead.

This silver cup was found, together with other grave goods, in a royal burial mound at Jelling, in Denmark.

YOU WILL NEED

Shaped plastic pot (eg empty dessert pot)

Tissue paper or kitchen towel

PVA glue & brush

Split peas & string

Scissors

Silver poster paint & brush

Black poster paint

SILVER VESSEL

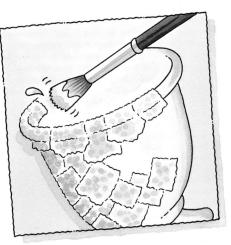

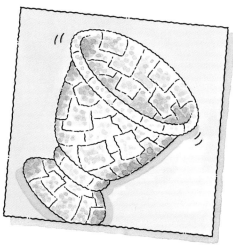

1. Clean the plastic pot before you start. Brush on PVA glue and then cover the pot with small pieces of torn tissue or paper towel.

2. Build up the layers of tissue, inside and outside the pot, to make the pot look thicker. The crumpled tissue gives the pot a rough textured surface.

3. Leave the pot in a safe place to dry. To make the raised pattern on the cup, glue the split peas to the surface with PVA.

4. Now glue lengths of string around the pot. The Vikings liked to use curved patterns and coiled shapes. These are easy to make with lengths of glued string.

5. Paint inside and outside the pot with silver poster paint. Darken the silver paint with black poster paint and lightly brush over the pot to give an aged appearance.

6. Try making other vessels by using plastic pots of different shapes and sizes. You can decorate them using other materials to give unusual raised designs and textures.

Try painting your hoard of treasure in gold or bronze paints.

GODS AND AMULETS

THE VIKINGS had a long tradition of storytelling. Few people could read, so stories of their gods were passed on by word of mouth. Their chief gods were **Odin**, **Thor** and **Frey**. Thor was the ruler of the sky and was popular with the farmers and peasants because he had power over the weather. He battled against evil by wielding his mighty hammer. Many Vikings wore **amulets** in the shape of Thor's hammer to protect them against evil. Everyone also wore jewellery, such as brooches and clasps, to keep their clothes fastened.

People who could afford to had very elaborate and beautiful jewellery made, and wore it to show their wealth and status.

AMULETS

YOU WILL NEED

Thick card & pencil
Craft knife & cutting board
PVA glue & brush
Tissue paper
Lengths of string

Scissors
Small buttons
& split peas
Gold poster paint
& brush

Hole punch

1. Draw the shape of Thor's hammer on thick card and cut it out carefully. Make a hole in the top with the hole punch. Start to cover the shape with glued pieces of tissue.

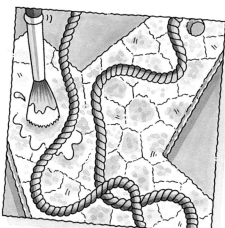

2. Build up layers of the glued tissue, covering the back and front of the shape. Make sure you leave the hole uncovered. Glue string onto the front of the shape in curved patterns.

3. Finish off the design by gluing the buttons and split peas in place. Leave to dry. Make sure everything is stuck down firmly before painting the amulet with gold poster paint.

24

ARM RINGS

The Vikings made beautiful jewellery from twisted lengths of silver and gold.

Men and women wore twisted gold around their arms and necks.

1. Make a ring of string by coiling a length of string several times and gluing it together with PVA. Leave the ring to dry.

2. Wrap a second length of string around the ring, keeping it as tight and twisted as you can. Glue it together with PVA and when it is dry paint it gold.

Try making different sized gold rings to wear around your arms.

Odin was the king of the gods. He was also called Woden. Wednesday was named in his honour. Thursday was named after Thor.

VIKING BOARD GAME

THE VIKINGS enjoyed games of skill and chance. They played games to relax and pass away the long winter evenings. A popular Viking game was 'hneftafl' (meaning the King's Table). This was played on a squared board with simple counters carved from wood and bone.

It is thought that the Vikings invented this game, but travellers could have brought it home from the East. Game boards, like the carved stone slab on the left, have been found far across the Viking world, from Ireland to the Ukraine.

These chessmen from the Isle of Lewis were made during the late Viking age.

HNEFTAFL GAME

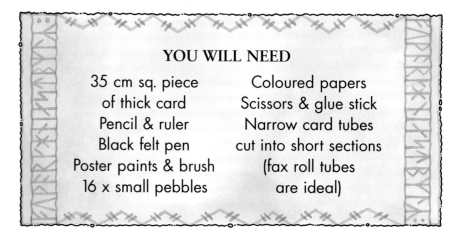

YOU WILL NEED

35 cm sq. piece of thick card	Coloured papers
Pencil & ruler	Scissors & glue stick
Black felt pen	Narrow card tubes
Poster paints & brush	cut into short sections
16 x small pebbles	(fax roll tubes are ideal)

1. Use the pencil and ruler to measure a 1cm border around the edge of the card square. Divide the rest of the board into 3cm squares. There will be 11 squares on each side.

2. Draw over the pencil grid with a black felt pen to make the lines thicker. Either colour in the board pattern or make a mosaic design using squares of coloured paper.

3. Follow the board design shown here. Make the paper squares slightly smaller than the squares on the grid and make sure the colours are in the correct places.

The aim of the game is for the attacking force to capture the King.

The King is in the centre of the board, surrounded by his 8 Vikings who will try to defend him.

The attacking force of 16 stone counters are positioned in groups of 4 around each side.

4. You will need an attacking force of 16 stone counters, a defence force of 8 Vikings and 1 King. The stone counters are similar sized pebbles, all painted the same colour.

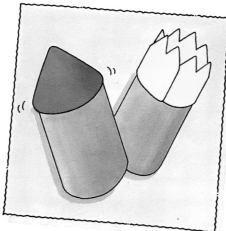

5. The Vikings and King are made from short lengths of tube. Paint the tubes. Make small paper cone helmets for the Vikings and a crown for the King and glue them in place.

The game is played like Draughts or Checkers. All the counters move one square at a time in any direction. Two players take it in turns to move their force one counter at a time. A counter can take one of the opposite force by jumping over it. If the attackers take the King they are the winners, if the defenders take all the attacking men then they are victorious!

Make or decorate a box to keep all the pieces in.

VIKING CHIEFTAINS

AT THE BEGINNING of the Viking age there were many chieftains and nobles. These individuals were landowners and warriors who ruled over small villages and communities, but they were all subject to the rule of 'the **Thing**' or local assembly, where laws and decisions were made.

Over time the most powerful chieftains increased their authority by raiding and conquering neighbouring lands, until vast areas of **Scandinavia** were controlled by just a few. Gradually the kings gained control, took away the nobles' powers and unified the countries.

This striking portrait of a Viking chieftain is carved from a single **elk** antler.

CHIEF BOXES

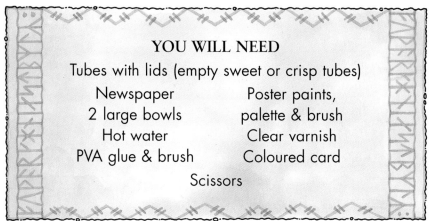

YOU WILL NEED

Tubes with lids (empty sweet or crisp tubes)

Newspaper	Poster paints,
2 large bowls	palette & brush
Hot water	Clear varnish
PVA glue & brush	Coloured card

Scissors

1. To make the paper pulp, tear up the newspaper into small pieces and put them in a large bowl. Cover the paper pieces with hot water and leave them to soak overnight.

2. Take handfuls of the wet paper, squeeze out all the water and place it in the second bowl. Then use your hands to mash it together with the PVA glue.

3. Take off the tube lid and begin to press small lumps of pulp to it, gradually building up a dome shape. Brush on extra PVA to help the pulp stick to the top of the lid.

4. Build up the conical Viking helmet and head shape, and add more pulp to form the nose and beard. Smooth over any lumps with your fingers and leave to dry.

5. Repeat the process with all the lids, making each a different character. When they are all dry, paint them and apply a couple of coats of clear varnish to protect them.

6. Paint the tubes with poster paints, drawing in details of the costumes and armour. Cut out shield shapes from card, decorate them and glue them to the body.

The Viking chieftain boxes make handy pencil boxes and desk tidies.

29

GLOSSARY

Amulet – A magic charm, which the wearer believes gives protection and good fortune.

Barter – A system of trading goods without using money, operated by swapping items of similar value.

Berserker – Fearless Viking warriors who worked themselves up into a mad state before battle. They fought naked apart from the bearskin clothes from which they got their name.

Chain mail – A suit of armour made from links of iron, expensive to make and usually worn by wealthy leaders. Sometimes a piece of chain mail was attached to the back of the helmet to protect the neck.

Elk – Largest of all deer, the elk is known as the moose in North America. Common in Scandinavia during the Viking age, it was hunted for its meat, skin and antlers.

Fjords – Water inlets along the Scandinavian coastline leading to the sea.

Frey – The Viking god of fertility, who was thought to bring the Vikings plentiful crops and many children. His sister, Freyja, was the goddess of love.

Hoard – Many Vikings kept their valuables buried in a secret place for safe keeping as there were no banks, and these places are called hoards. Many Vikings died in battle or forgot where they had buried their hoard. Their treasure is still being discovered today.

Jorvik – Now the modern day city of York in Great Britain. Jorvik was a major trading centre for the Vikings during the 10th century AD.

Keel – The ship's backbone. In Viking ships the keel was made from one piece of oak and the rest of the ship was built on to it.

Longship – A long, narrow ship used by the Vikings for sea voyages of exploration and for warfare.

Odin – The Viking god of war and wisdom. He was one of the chief gods and had many supernatural powers.

Rigging – The ropes used to tie a ship's sail to the mast.

Runes – The characters of the 'futhark', the Viking alphabet, which has 16 symbols. These were carved on wood, bone and stone, and never written with pen and ink.

Runestone – A memorial stone carved with runes.

Sagas – Legends about heroes and gods, told by the Scandinavian poets called 'skalds', and storytellers.

Scandinavia – The Viking homeland that was divided into kingdoms, and led eventually to the development of the independent nations of Norway, Sweden, Denmark and Iceland.

Ship graves – Important Vikings were often buried in ships, in the belief that they would sail to an afterlife. The ships were buried under mounds or set on fire at sea.

Starboard – A nautical term meaning the right side of a ship, from the steering board or rudder that was always attached to the right side. Port is the left side of the ship.

Stern – The rear end of a ship. The front is called the prow, and this was often decorated with carved dragon heads.

Sun compass – A navigational tool used by the Vikings. From a cast shadow the height of the sun above the horizon could be measured, making it possible to calculate latitude, ie the north/south position.

Thing – A Viking assembly of free men, where important matters were discussed and laws were passed.

Thor – The Viking god of thunder, the son of Odin.

INDEX

A
alphabet 8
amulets 24-5
animals 6

B
barter 18, 20
berserkers 17
blacksmiths 6
board games 26-7
bookends 8-9
boxes 28-9
brooches 6, 24
burials 4, 5, 22-3

C
carvings 4, 5, 6, 9, 14,
    26, 28
chain mail 16
chess 26
chieftains 5, 22, 28-9
clasps 6, 24
coiled patterns 15, 23
coins 18, 19-20
collage 7, 23

D
Denmark 4, 5
die stamps 19-20
dowels 7
dragons 4, 9, 14-15

E
elk 28

F
figureheads 14
fjords 10
freemen 5
Frey 24
futhark 8

G
gods 24

H
head-posts 4
helmets 16-17
hneftafl game 26-7
hoards 22-3

J
jewellery 6, 8, 14, 24-5
Jorvik 20

K
keel 10

L
longships 10-11, 14-15

M
mast 10
materials 7
metal 6
metallic paints 7

N
navigation 12-13
nobles 5, 22, 28
Norway 4, 5

O
oars 10
Odin 24

R
ravens 12, 14
rigging 11
rudder 11
runes 6, 8-9
runestones 4, 6, 8-9

S
sagas 12, 14
sails 10-11
scales 18-19
Scandinavia 4, 8, 10,
    18, 28
serpents 9
shields 11
ship graves 22
ships 4, 6, 10
silver 18, 20, 22
slaves 5, 18
sun compasses 12-13
Sweden 4, 5

T
Thing 5, 28
Thor 24
thralls 5
treasure 22-3

W
warriors 16-17
wood 16-17
writing 6, 8-9